San Francisco's
1906 EARTHQUAKE

A BOOK OF POSTCARDS

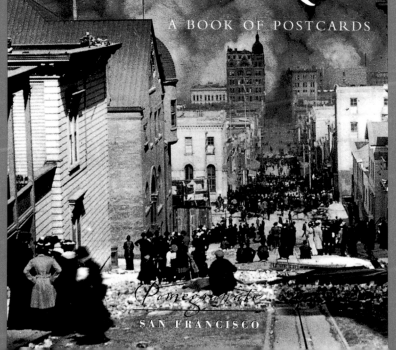

Pomegranate

SAN FRANCISCO

Pomegranate Communications, Inc.
Box 808022, Petaluma, California 94975
800-227-1428
www.pomegranate.com

Pomegranate Europe Ltd.
Unit 1, Heathcote Business Centre, Hurlbutt Road
Warwick, Warwickshire CV34 6TD, U.K.
[+44] 0 1926 430111

ISBN 0-7649-2948-8
Pomegranate Catalog No. AA261

Pomegranate publishes books of
postcards on a wide range of subjects.
Please contact the publisher for more information.

Cover designed by Lisa Alban
Printed in China
13 12 11 10 09 08 07 06 05 04   10 9 8 7 6 5 4 3 2 1

To facilitate detachment of the postcards from this book, fold each card along its perforation line before tearing.

At 5:12 A.M. on April 18, 1906, an earthquake of extraordinary violence hurled the luckier San Franciscans from their beds. Hundreds of the luckless were crushed as downtown and South of Market buildings fell in upon themselves. The quake—magnitude roughly 7.9, duration 45 to 60 seconds, depending on location—was quickly followed by dozens of fires started by toppled oil lamps and ruptured gas lines. Ruptures also occurred in the city's water mains, rendering firefighters helpless. The fires spread uncontested until they converged in an immense firestorm that devoured San Francisco, laying waste to thousands of acres and taking thousands of lives. (Estimates of the number of dead are inexact: City Hall records were lost the first day of the fire, and the welding-temperature blaze completely incinerated many of its victims.)

As catastrophes tend to do, the earthquake and fire aroused a surge of altruism and public spirit in the city's citizens. The newly homeless were housed in tents provided by the army. (From the quake's first minutes, General Frederick Funston acted quickly, intelligently, and heroically to keep the peace and to care for the citizenry.) In a matter of days the vast expanses of rubble were heaped to make the city navigable once more, and before long San Francisco began to rise again.

San Francisco's 1906 EARTHQUAKE

Golden Gate Avenue and Larkin Street
Photograph: California Historical Society, FN-36066

BOX 808022　PETALUMA　CA 94975

Pomegranate

San Francisco's 1906 EARTHQUAKE

Hibernia Bank

Photograph: California Historical Society, FN-36067

BOX 808022   PETALUMA   CA 94975

Pomegranate

San Francisco's 1906 EARTHQUAKE

View from Russian Hill
Photograph by Arnold Genthe
California Historical Society, FN-21127

BOX 808022   PETALUMA   CA 94975

Pomegranate

San Francisco's 1906 EARTHQUAKE

Downtown ruins
Photograph: California Historical Society, FN-28544

BOX 808022 PETALUMA CA 94975

Pomegranate

San Francisco's 1906 EARTHQUAKE

City Hall

Photograph: California Historical Society, FN-36064

BOX 808022   PETALUMA   CA 94975

Pomegranate

San Francisco's 1906 EARTHQUAKE

Union Square

Photograph: California Historical Society, FN-34304

BOX 808022   PETALUMA   CA 94975

Pomegranate

San Francisco's 1906 EARTHQUAKE

Majestic Theatre, 1281 Market Street

Photograph: California Historical Society, FN-28963

BOX 808022   PETALUMA   CA 94975

Pomegranate

San Francisco's 1906 EARTHQUAKE

The Oyster Loaf and Chat Noir, 1617 Oak Street
Photograph: California Historical Society, FN-33958

BOX 808022   PETALUMA   CA 94975

Pomegranate

BEAR PHOTO
S.F. 355

San Francisco's 1906 EARTHQUAKE

Native Sons monument, on Market at Turk and Mason
Photograph: California Historical Society, FN-36055

BOX 808022   PETALUMA   CA 94975

Pomegranate

San Francisco's 1906 EARTHQUAKE

Portsmouth Square and Hall of Justice
Photograph: California Historical Society, FN-36058

BOX 808022 PETALUMA CA 94975

Pomegranate

San Francisco's 1906 EARTHQUAKE

Jones Street, California to Sacramento

Photograph: California Historical Society, FN-36059

BOX 808022   PETALUMA   CA 94975

Pomegranate

San Francisco's 1906 EARTHQUAKE

Van Ness Avenue, Bush to Pine Streets
Photograph: California Historical Society, FN-34901

BOX 808022 PETALUMA CA 94975

Pomegranate

BEAR PHOTO
S.F. 72.

San Francisco's 1906 EARTHQUAKE

Car tracks on Vallejo Street
Photograph: California Historical Society, FN-36060

BOX 808022 PETALUMA CA 94975

Pomegranate

San Francisco's 1906 EARTHQUAKE

Union Street damage
Photograph: California Historical Society, FN-34881

BOX 808022 PETALUMA CA 94975

Pomegranate

San Francisco's 1906 EARTHQUAKE

Palace Hotel entrance on New Montgomery Street
Photograph: California Historical Society, FN-36062

BOX 808022   PETALUMA   CA 94975

Pomegranate

San Francisco's 1906 EARTHQUAKE

Union Iron Works, Pier 70
Photograph: California Historical Society, FN-36057

BOX 808022 PETALUMA CA 94975

Pomegranate

San Francisco's 1906 EARTHQUAKE

The Market Street Bank
Photograph: California Historical Society, FN-36056

BOX 808022 PETALUMA CA 94975

Pomegranate

San Francisco's 1906 EARTHQUAKE

San Francisco Examiner Building, 3rd and Market
Photograph: California Historical Society, FN-36068

BOX 808022 PETALUMA CA 94975

Pomegranate

San Francisco's 1906 EARTHQUAKE

Refugee camp below Fort Mason
Photograph: California Historical Society, FN-25438

BOX 808022   PETALUMA   CA 94975

Pomegranate

San Francisco's 1906 EARTHQUAKE

Sutter Street, between Mason and Taylor
Photograph: California Historical Society, FN-23448

BOX 808022   PETALUMA   CA 94975

Pomegranate

San Francisco's 1906 EARTHQUAKE

Market Street burning, as seen from Stockton Street
Photograph: California Historical Society, FN-26615

BOX 808022 PETALUMA CA 94975

Pomegranate

San Francisco's 1906 EARTHQUAKE

Police depot in Portsmouth Square
Photograph: California Historical Society, FN-27594

BOX 808022 PETALUMA CA 94975

Pomegranate

San Francisco's 1906 EARTHQUAKE

Crack in the street

Photograph: California Historical Society, FN-26472

BOX 808022   PETALUMA   CA 94975

Pomegranate

San Francisco's 1906 EARTHQUAKE

Jackson Brewery, Folsom at 11th Street, May 19, 1906
Photograph: California Historical Society, FN-29227

BOX 808022   PETALUMA   CA 94975

Pomegranate

San Francisco's 1906 EARTHQUAKE

Spreckels Bandstand, Golden Gate Park
Photograph: California Historical Society, FN-12770

BOX 808022   PETALUMA   CA 94975

Pomegranate

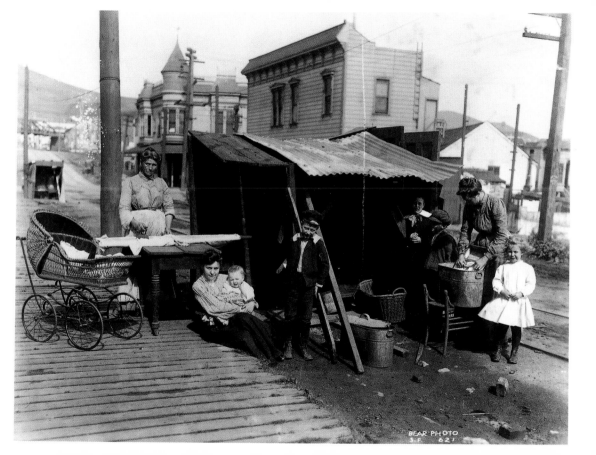

BEAR PHOTO
S.F. 621

San Francisco's 1906 EARTHQUAKE

Life in the street
Photograph: California Historical Society, FN-17808

BOX 808022 PETALUMA CA 94975

Pomegranate

San Francisco's 1906 EARTHQUAKE

Fairmont Hotel from Jones Street
Photograph: California Historical Society, FN-02599

BOX 808022 PETALUMA CA 94975

San Francisco's 1906 EARTHQUAKE

Capp Street at 17th Street
Photograph: California Historical Society, FN-02597

BOX 808022 PETALUMA CA 94975

Pomegranate

San Francisco's 1906 EARTHQUAKE

Refugees dining on Franklin Street near Fulton
Photograph: California Historical Society, GN-1404

BOX 808022 PETALUMA CA 94975

Pomegranate

San Francisco's 1906 EARTHQUAKE

Looking down Sacramento Street, April 18, 1906
Photograph by Arnold Genthe
Photograph: California Historical Society, FN-04024

BOX 808022 PETALUMA CA 94975

Pomegranate